EXTREME WEATHER

FLOOD

Norwood House Press

JACK WILLIAMS

Cataloging-in-Publication Data

Names: Williams, Jack.
Title: Floods / Jack WIlliams.
Description: Buffalo, NY : Norwood House Press, 2026. | Series: Extreme weather | Includes glossary and index.
Identifiers: ISBN 9781978576742 (pbk.) | ISBN 9781978576759 (library bound) | ISBN 9781978576766 (ebook)
Subjects: LCSH: Floods--Juvenile literature.
Classification: LCC GB1399.W555 2026 | DDC 363.3493--dc23

Published in 2026 by
Norwood House Press
2544 Clinton Street
Buffalo, NY 14224

Designer: Rhea Magaro
Editor: Kim Thompson

Photo credits: Cover, p1. Jaroslav Moravcik, Janis Abolins /Shutterstock.com; p. 5 elmar gubisch/Shutterstock.com; p. 6 Bilanol/Shutterstock.com; p. 8 Adam bartosik/Shutterstock.com; p. 10 JuShoot/Shutterstock.com; p. 12 wk1003mike/Shutterstock.com; p. 13 Ivan Ventura/Shutterstock.com; p. 14 Ajdin Kamber/Shutterstock.com; p. 15 Anelo/Shutterstock.com; p. 16 michelmond/Shutterstock.com; p. 19 sirirak kaewgorn/Shutterstock.com; p. 20 Nicole Glass Photography/Shutterstock.com

Printed in the United States of America

TABLE OF CONTENTS

WATCH OUT!

Water rushes. It spreads. It rises.

Watch out! It is a **flood**.

WHAT IS A FLOOD?

In a flood, water flows in places that are usually dry.

Floods can last hours, days, or weeks.

Soil soaks up water.

Sometimes, there is too much water. The soil cannot **absorb** it all.

Rivers and streams **overflow**.

Water spills over their **banks**.

There can be floods when there is lots of rain.

There can be floods when storms push water from the ocean onto the land.

WHY ARE FLOODS DANGEROUS?

Moving water is a powerful **force**. It can wash away cars and buildings.

Just six inches (15 centimeters) of rushing water can knock a person down.

3602

Floodwater can **ruin** people's things.

Germs in the water can make people sick.

HOW TO STAY SAFE

Pay attention to the weather **forecast**.

A flood warning means that a flood could happen.

FLOOD
WARNING!

ROAD
CLOSED

Move to a high floor of your home.

Follow directions. You may need to **evacuate**.

Never walk, swim, or drive through floodwater.

GLOSSARY

absorb (ab-ZORB): to soak up liquid like a sponge

banks (bangks): the sloping land along the sides of a river, stream, or creek

evacuate (i-VAK-yoo-ate): to leave a place quickly because of danger

flood (fluhd): the rising and overflowing of water onto land that is normally dry

force (fors): a push or pull that can move things

forecast (FOR-kast): a report that tells what the weather will be like in the future

germs (jurmz): tiny living things that can make you sick

overflow (oh-vur-FLOH): to spill over the top or edges of something

ruin (ROO-in): to damage something so badly it cannot be used anymore

soil (soil): the dirt that covers Earth's surface

THINKING QUESTIONS

1. How long can a flood last?
2. How does soil help control water?
3. Describe two ways that floods can harm people.
4. What is a flood warning?
5. What shouldn't you do during a flood?

INDEX

ABOUT THE AUTHOR

Jack Williams is curious about all things in nature, especially the weather! He checks the weather forecast every day. He used to be a police officer, so he knows how important it is to watch out for danger and stay safe.